PIANO SOLO
ULTIMATE NEW AGE

• 39 OF THE BEST CONTEMPORARY INSTRUMENTALS •

Page	Title	Artist
2	Angel's Flight	SHADOWFAX
14	Anne's Song	WILLIAM ACKERMAN
7	Barcelona	JOHN TESH
20	The Carriage Road	JIM CHAPPELL
24	Cast Your Fate to the Wind	GEORGE WINSTON
36	Celestial Soda Pop	RAY LYNCH
33	Chariots of Fire	VANGELIS
44	Country Night	GEORGE WINSTON
47	Cristofori's Dream	DAVID LANZ
56	A Day to Remember	JONATHAN CAIN
64	A Day Without Rain	ENYA
66	Devotion	LIZ STORY
70	Earthrise/Return	MANNHEIM STEAMROLLER
80	Engravings	IRA STEIN
86	First Kiss	DAVID ARKENSTONE
90	Flowers on the Water	KOSTIA
106	Freedom	JIM BRICKMAN
112	Gone	JIM CHAPPELL
118	Homeland	TINGSTAD AND RUMBEL
124	The Last Snow Leopard	SPENCER BREWER
128	Lullaby	JIM CHAPPELL
132	Madrona	DAVID LANZ
136	The Memory of Trees	ENYA
140	Montana Half-light	PHILIP AABERG
97	No Blue Thing	RAY LYNCH
146	Ocean Suite (Part 1)	STEVEN HALPERN
149	Rain on the Pond	WAYNE GRATZ
154	Return to the Heart	DAVID LANZ
158	Solid Colors	LIZ STORY
168	The Steamroller	MANNHEIM STEAMROLLER
177	Sunrise	MICHAEL JONES
184	Sunshine Canyon	MICHAEL JONES
198	Tubular Bells	MIKE OLDFIELD
202	Valley in the Clouds	DAVID ARKENSTONE
208	The Velocity of Love	SUZANNE CIANI
189	Vincent (Starry, Starry Night)	LORIE LINE
214	Volver, Volver	RICHARD CLAYDERMAN
220	Watermark	ENYA
222	Winter Waltz	KITARO

ISBN 0-634-08651-0

HAL•LEONARD® CORPORATION

7777 W. BLUEMOUND RD. P.O. BOX 13819 MILWAUKEE, WI 53213

For all works contained herein:
Unauthorized copying, arranging, adapting, recording or public performance is an infringement of copyright.
Infringers are liable under the law.

Visit Hal Leonard Online at
www.halleonard.com

ANGEL'S FLIGHT

By CHUCK GREENBERG

BARCELONA

Music by JOHN TESH

Copyright © 1992 Teshmusic (BMI)
International Copyright Secured   All Rights Reserved

ANNE'S SONG

By WILLIAM ACKERMAN

Copyright © 1979 Imaginary Road Music (BMI)
All Rights Reserved   Used by Permission

Lilting, rhythmic

THE CARRIAGE ROAD

By JIM CHAPPELL

Copyright © 1996 Unspeakable Freedom Music (BMI)
International Copyright Secured   All Rights Reserved

CAST YOUR FATE TO THE WIND

Words and Music by VINCE GUARALDI
and CAREL WERVER

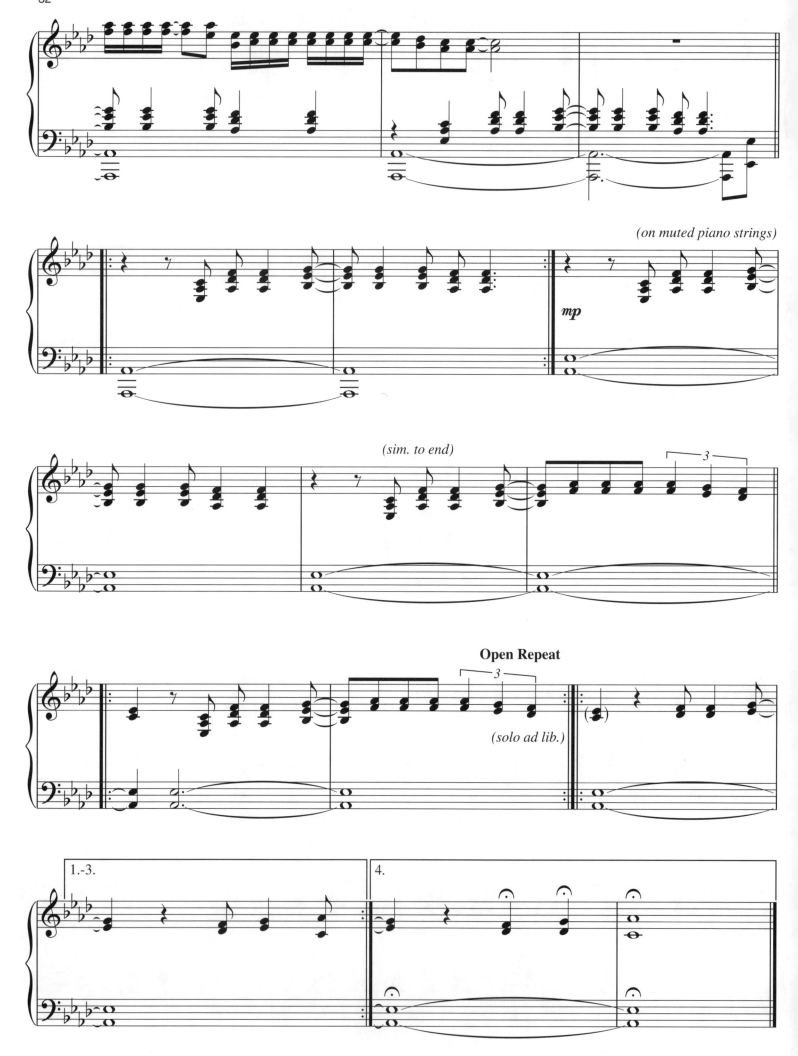

CHARIOTS OF FIRE

Music by VANGELIS

CELESTIAL SODA POP

Composed by RAY LYNCH

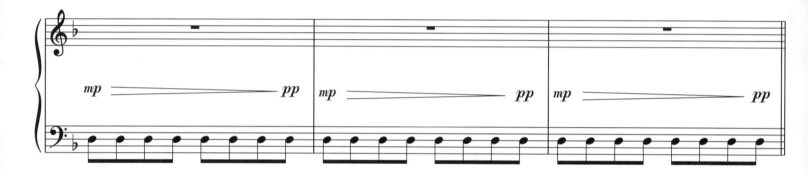

Copyright © 1984, 1985 Ray Lynch Productions, 10336 Loch Lomond Rd., PMB 118, Middletown, CA 95461-9500 www.raylynch.com
International Copyright Secured   All Rights Reserved

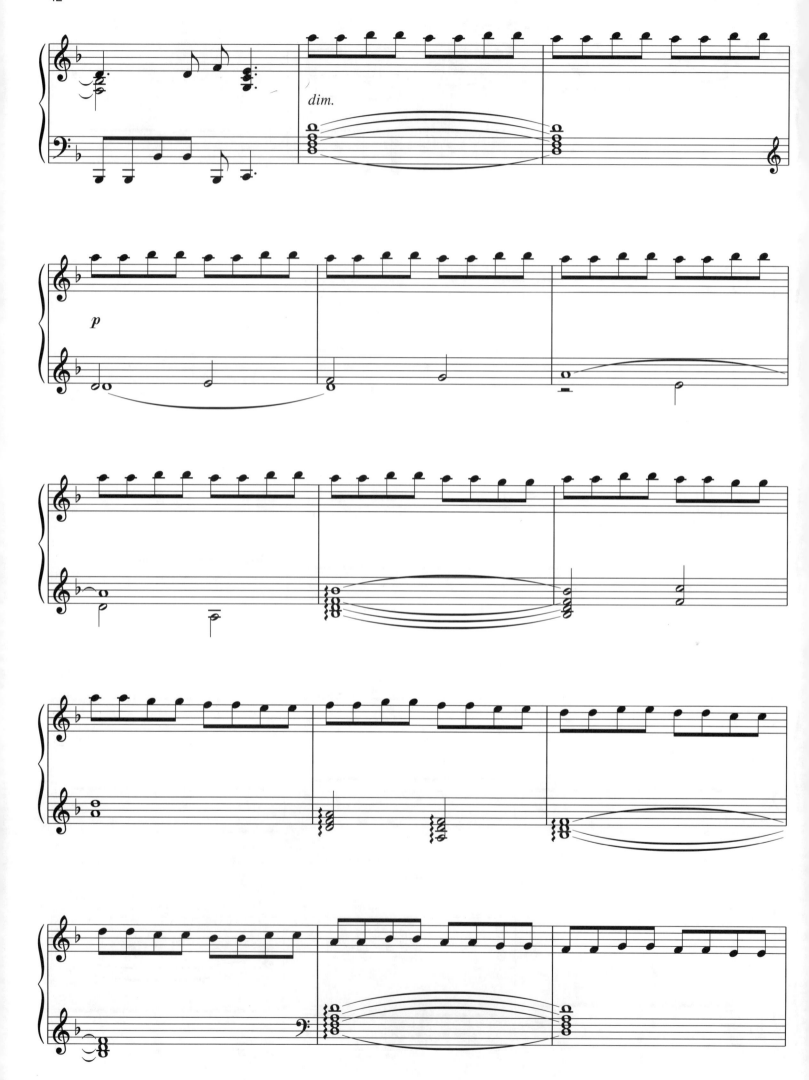

COUNTRY NIGHT

By CHARLES GROSS
and GEORGE WINSTON

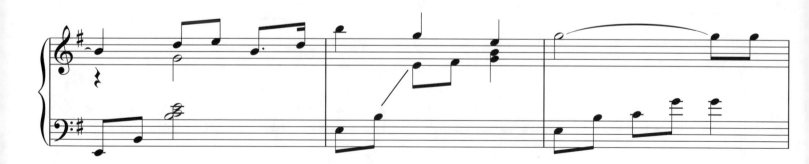

© 1984 Touchstone Pictures Music & Songs, Inc. and Buena Vista Music
All Rights Reserved   Used by Permission

CRISTOFORI'S DREAM

By DAVID LANZ

© 1988 Nara Music, Inc. (BMI)
4650 North Port Washington Road, Milwaukee, WI 53212
All Rights Reserved

A DAY TO REMEMBER

Written by JONATHAN CAIN

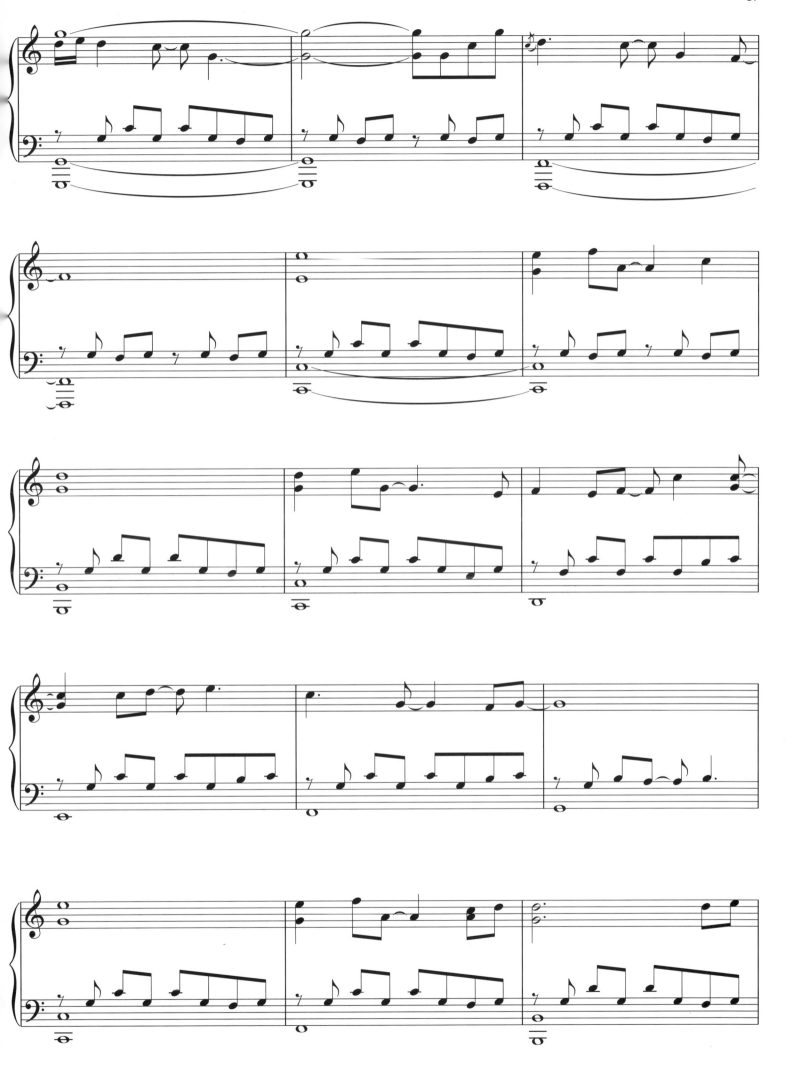

A DAY WITHOUT RAIN

By ENYA and NICKY RYAN

© 2000, 2001 EMI MUSIC PUBLISHING LTD.
All Rights in the U.S. and Canada Controlled and Administered by EMI BLACKWOOD MUSIC INC.
All Rights Reserved   International Copyright Secured   Used by Permission

DEVOTION

By LIZ STORY

* 12/8 and 9/8 in this piece remain in *duple* meter
(the beat is subdivided by two).

69

EARTHRISE/RETURN

By CHIP DAVIS

Copyright © 1983 by Dots and Lines Ink
All Rights Reserved Including Public Performance For Profit

RETURN

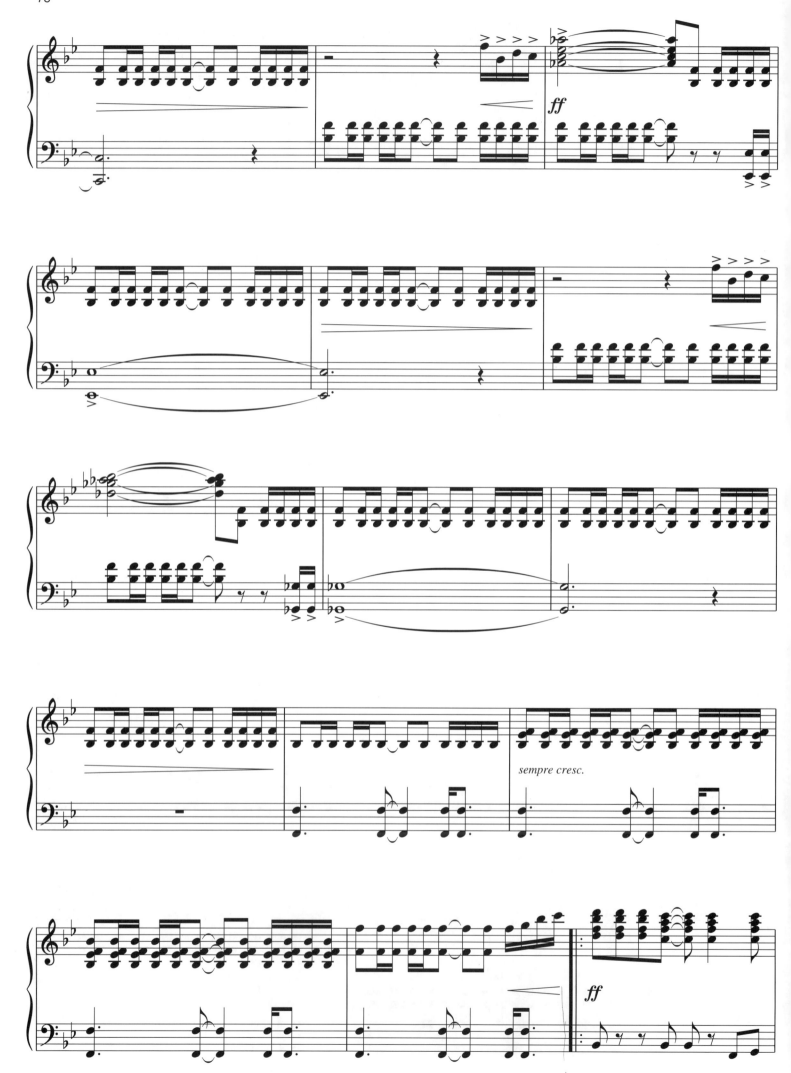

ENGRAVINGS

By IRA STEIN

Copyright © 1986 Lost Time Music (BMI) and Imaginary Roads Music (BMI)
All Rights Administered by Windham Hill Music (BMI)
International Copyright Secured   All Rights Reserved

FIRST KISS

By DAVID ARKENSTONE

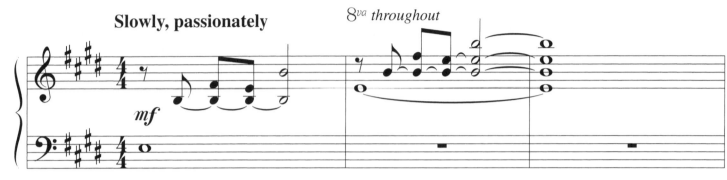

© 1994 Nara Music, Inc. (BMI)
4650 North Port Washington Road
Milwaukee, WI 53212-1063
All Rights Reserved

FLOWERS ON THE WATER

By KOSTIA

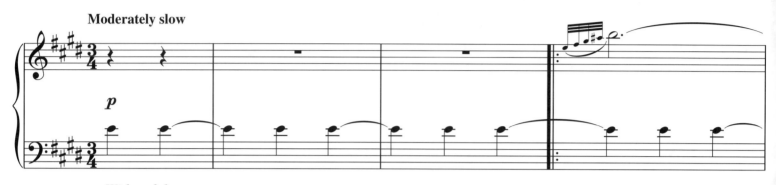
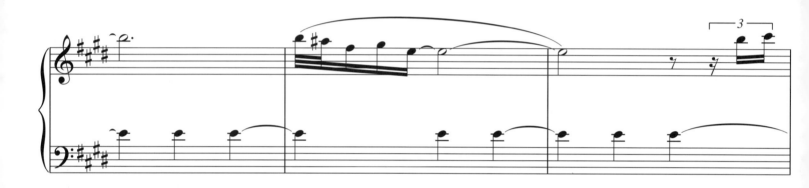
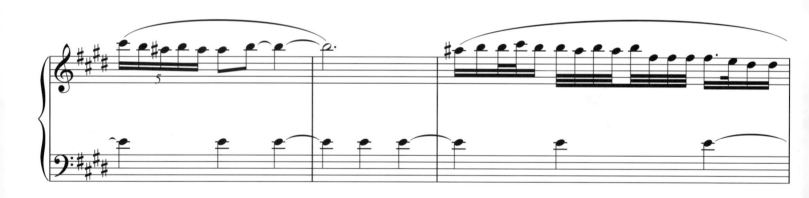

© 1992 Nara Music Inc.
4650 N. Port Washington Road, Milwaukee, WI 53212
All Rights Reserved

NO BLUE THING

Composed by RAY LYNCH

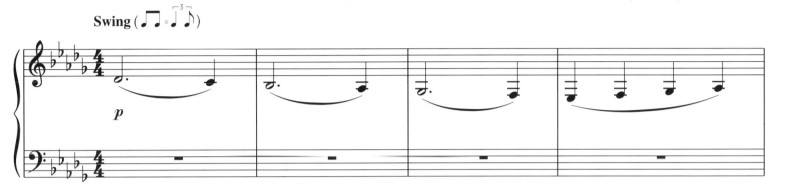
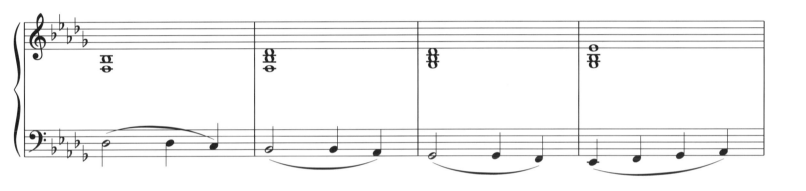

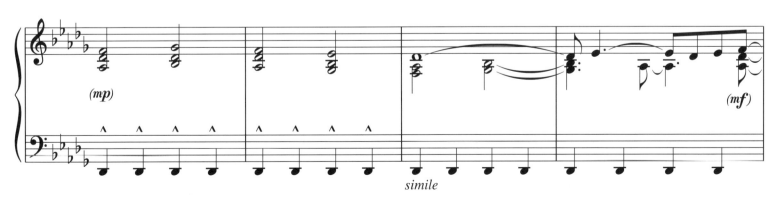

FREEDOM

By JIM BRICKMAN

GONE

By JIM CHAPPELL

Copyright © 1987 Unspeakable Freedom Music (BMI)
International Copyright Secured   All Rights Reserved

HOMELAND

By ERIC TINGSTAD

Open Repeat (solo ad lib.)

dim.

(oboe solo as in opening)

mp

(bass line fades away to nothing)

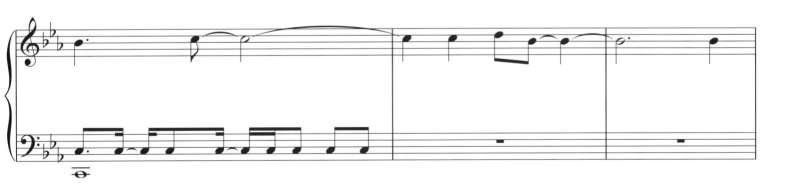

THE LAST SNOW LEOPARD

By SPENCER BREWER

© 1986 Nara Music, Inc.
4650 North Port Washington Road, Milwaukee, WI 53212
All Rights Reserved

LULLABY

By JIM CHAPPELL

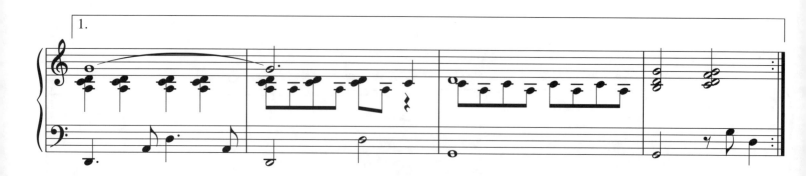

Copyright © 1990 Unspeakable Freedom Music (BMI)
International Copyright Secured   All Rights Reserved

MADRONA

By DAVID LANZ

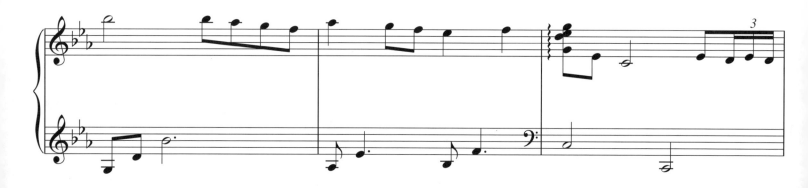

© 1987 Nara Music, Inc. (BMI)
4650 North Port Washington Road, Milwaukee, WI 53212
All Rights Reserved

THE MEMORY OF TREES

By ENYA
and NICKY RYAN

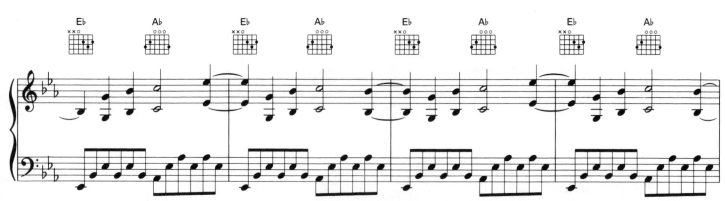

© 1995 EMI MUSIC PUBLISHING LTD.
All Rights Controlled and Administered by EMI BLACKWOOD MUSIC INC.
All Rights Reserved   International Copyright Secured   Used by Permission

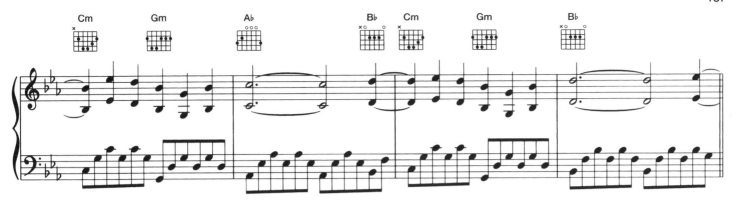
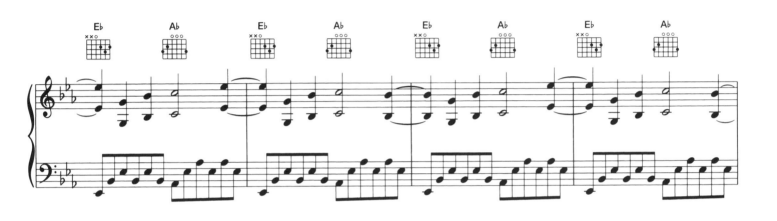

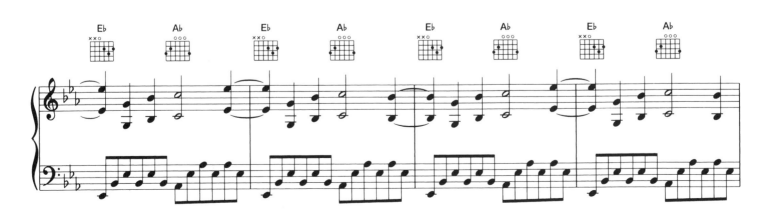

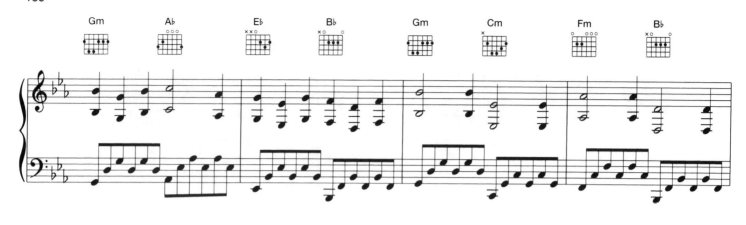
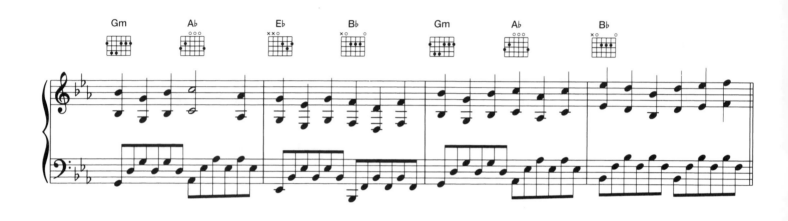
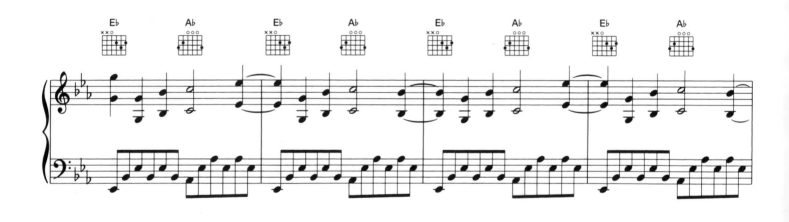
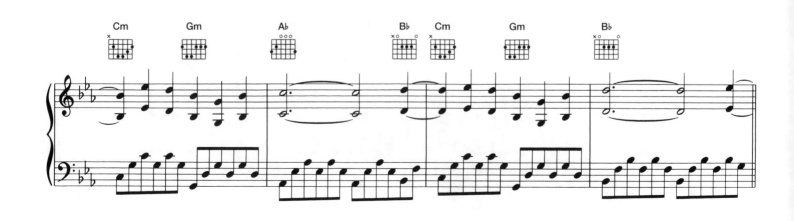

MONTANA HALF-LIGHT

By PHILIP AABERG

Like a deer in the headlights

Copyright © 1985 Beautiful Daughter Music (ASCAP)
All Rights Administered by Lost Lake Arts Music (ASCAP)
International Copyright Secured   All Rights Reserved

OCEAN SUITE
(Part 1)

By STEVEN HALPERN

Slow

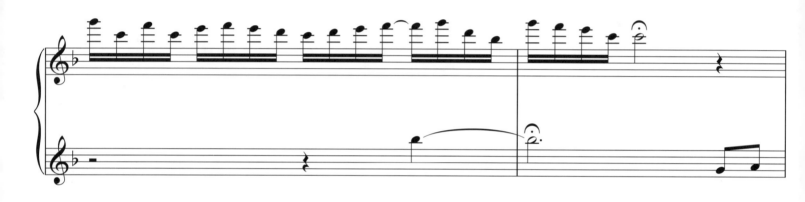

RAIN ON THE POND

By WAYNE GRATZ

© 1989 Nara Music, Inc. (BMI)
4650 North Port Washington Road, Milwaukee, WI 53212
All Rights Reserved

RETURN TO THE HEART

By DAVID LANZ

© 1991 Nara Music, Inc. (BMI)
4650 North Port Washington Road, Milwaukee, WI 53212
All Rights Reserved

SOLID COLORS

By LIZ STORY

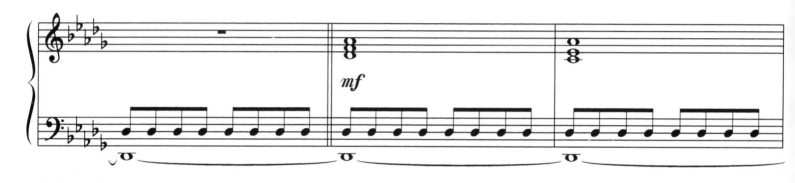

Copyright © 1983 Imaginary Roads Music (BMI)
All Rights Administered by Windham Hill Music (BMI)
International Copyright Secured   All Rights Reserved

THE STEAMROLLER

By CHIP DAVIS

SUNRISE

By MICHAEL JONES

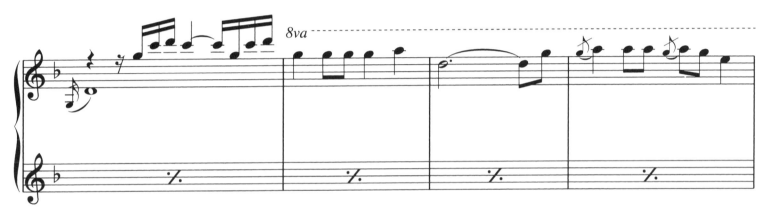

© 1990 Nara Music, Inc.
4650 N. Port Washington Road, Milwaukee, WI 53212
All Rights Reserved

SUNSHINE CANYON

By MICHAEL JONES
and DAVID DARLING

© 1987 Nara Music, Inc.
4650 North Port Washington Road, Milwaukee, WI 53212
All Rights Reserved

185

To Coda ⊕

(melody loco)

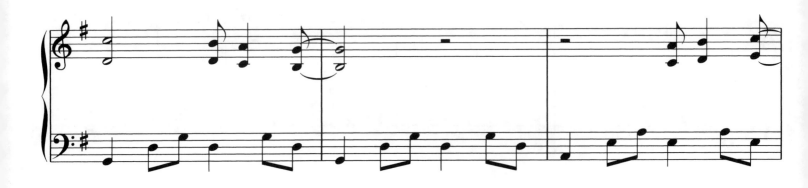

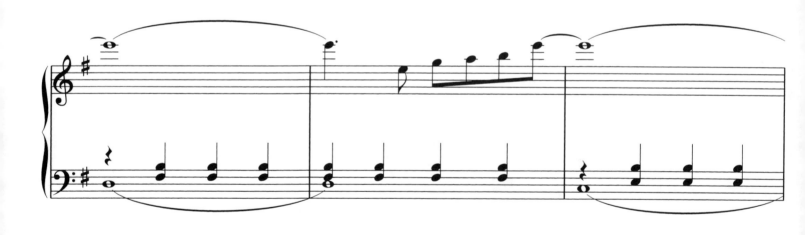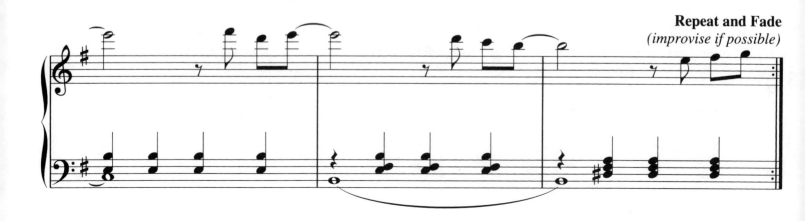

VINCENT
(Starry Starry Night)

Words and Music by
DON McLEAN

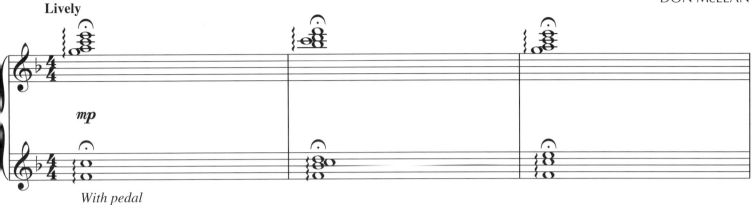
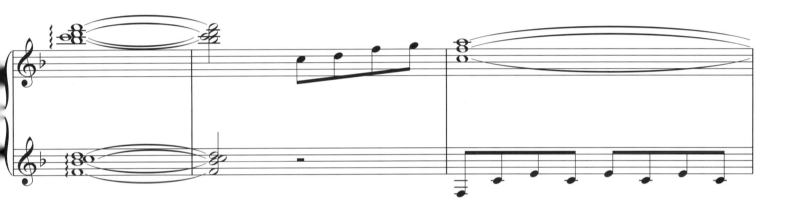

Copyright © 1971, 1972 BENNY BIRD CO., INC.
Copyrights Renewed
All Rights Controlled and Administered by SONGS OF UNIVERSAL, INC.
All Rights Reserved   Used by Permission

TUBULAR BELLS

By MIKE OLDFIELD

© 1974 (Renewed 2002) EMI VIRGIN MUSIC LTD.
All Rights for the U.S.A. and Canada Controlled and Administered by EMI VIRGIN MUSIC, INC.
All Rights Reserved   International Copyright Secured   Used by Permission

200

VALLEY IN THE CLOUDS

By DAVID ARKENSTONE

Light Reggae Feel

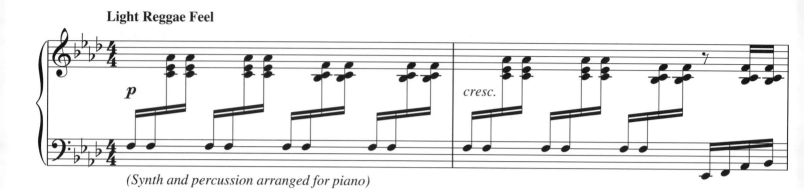

(Synth and percussion arranged for piano)

© 1987 Nara Music Inc.
4650 N. Port Washington Road, Milwaukee, WI 53212
All Rights Reserved

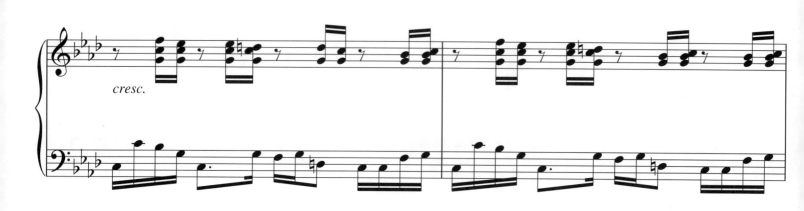

THE VELOCITY OF LOVE

By SUZANNE CIANI

Copyright © 1983 MUSICA INTERNATIONAL INC.
Published worldwide by MUSICA INTERNATIONAL INC.
International Copyright Secured   All Rights Reserved

210

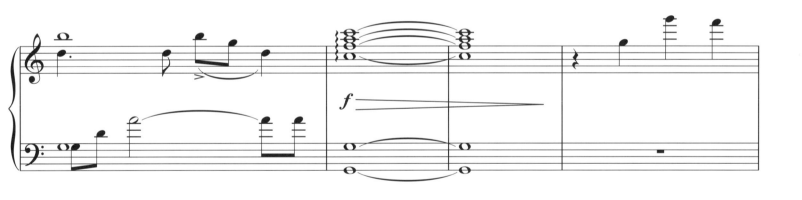

VOLVER, VOLVER

Words and Music by
FERNANDO Z. MALDONADO

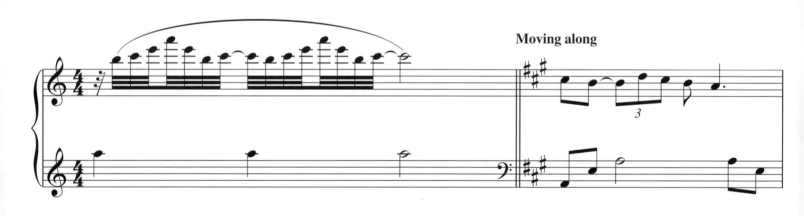

WINTER WALTZ

By MASANORI TAKAHASHI

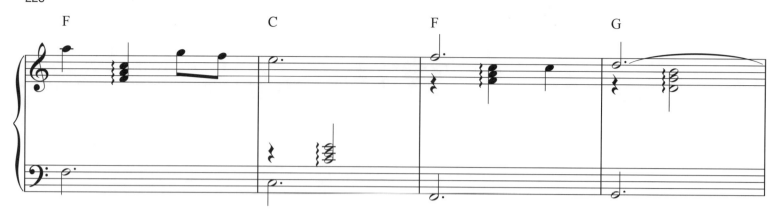
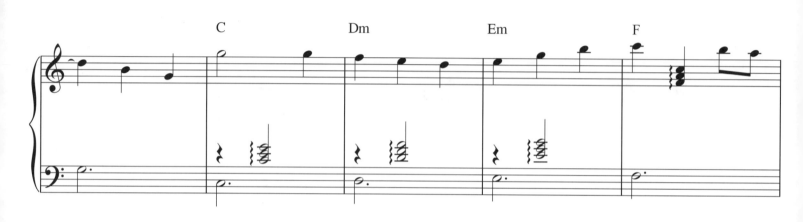
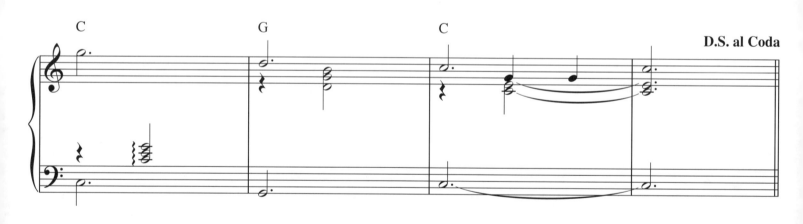

Your Favorite Music

Arranged For Piano Solo

Broadway – 20 Piano Solos
Play rich piano solo arrangements of 20 Broadway favorites! Includes: All I Ask of You • And All That Jazz • Can You Feel the Love Tonight • Edelweiss • The Impossible Dream • Memory • On My Own • Put On a Happy Face • Seasons of Love • Some Enchanted Evening • Summer Nights • Tomorrow • Unexpected Song • and more!
00311028 ....$12.95

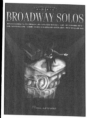
Classic Broadway Solos
16 beautifully arranged Broadway standards including: I Could Have Danced All Night • If Ever I Would Leave You • The Impossible Dream • Memory • Smoke Gets in Your Eyes • You'll Never Walk Alone • and more.
00294002 ....$12.95

Classical Themes from the Movies
Over 31 familiar and favorite themes, including: Also Sprach Zarathustra • Ave Maria • Canon in D • Habanera • Overture to *The Marriage of Figaro* • and more.
00221010 ....$9.95

Definitive Classical Collection
129 selections. Includes music by Johann Sebastian Bach, Ludwig van Beethoven, Johannes Brahms, Frederic Chopin, Claude Debussy, George Frideric Handel, Felix Mendelssohn, Johann Pachelbel, Franz Schubert, Pyotr Tchaikovsky, Richard Wagner, and many more!
00310772 ....$29.95

Jazz Standards
15 all-time favorite songs, including: All The Things You Are • Bluesette • I'll Remember April • Mood Indigo • Satin Doll • and more.
00292055 ....$12.95

Billy Joel Easy Classics
This unique collection includes 17 of his best songs: Honesty • It's Still Rock and Roll to Me • The Longest Time • Movin' Out (Anthony's Song) • My Life • Piano Man • Roberta • She's Got a Way • Uptown Girl • more.
00306202 ....$12.95

Lennon & McCartney Piano Solos
22 beautiful arrangements, including: Eleanor Rigby • The Fool on the Hill • Here, There and Everywhere • Lady Madonna • Let It Be • Yesterday • and more.
00294023 ....$14.95

Andrew Lloyd Webber
14 pieces, including: All I Ask of You • Don't Cry for Me Argentina • Memory • The Music of the Night • Phantom of the Opera • Pie Jesu • and more.
00292001 ....$14.95

Love & Wedding Piano Solos
26 contemporary and classic wedding favorites, including: All I Ask of You • Ave Maria • Endless Love • Through the Years • Vision of Love • Sunrise, Sunset • Don't Know Much • Unchained Melody • and more.
00311507 ....$12.95

Memorable Jazz Standards
24 elegant favorites: Autumn in New York • Autumn Leaves • Body and Soul • How Deep Is the Ocean • Isn't It Romantic? • It Might as Well Be Spring • My Funny Valentine • Satin Doll • Stella by Starlight • The Very Thought of You • When I Fall in Love • more.
00310719 ....$12.95

Movie Piano Solos
20 rich arrangements, including: The Exodus Song • The Firm Main Title • The Godfather (Love Theme) • Moon River • Raider's March • Theme From Schindler's List • When I Fall in Love • A Whole New World • and more.
00311675 ....$10.95

Elvis Presley Pianos Solos
A great collection of over 15 of The King's best, including: Are You Lonesome Tonight? • Don't Be Cruel • It's Now or Never • Love Me Tender • All Shook Up • and more.
00292002 ....$9.95

Sacred Inspirations
arr. Phillip Keveren
11 songs, featuring: How Majestic Is Your Name • Great Is the Lord • Amazing Grace • Friends • Via Dolorosa • In the Name of the Lord • and more.
00292057 ....$9.95

Shout to the Lord
Moving arrangements of 14 praise favorites as interpreted by Phillip Keveren: As the Deer • El Shaddai • How Beautiful • How Majestic Is Your Name • More Precious Than Silver • Oh Lord, You're Beautiful • Shine, Jesus, Shine • Shout to the Lord • and more.
00310699 ....$12.95

Showcase for Piano
Intermediate to advanced arrangements of 18 popular songs: Bali Ha'i • Bewitched • I Can't Get Started with You • I Could Write a Book • I'll Be Seeing You • My Funny Valentine • September Song • Where or When • You'll Never Walk Alone • and more.
00310664 ....$8.95

TV Themes
33 classic themes, including: Addams Family • Alfred Hitchcock Presents • The Brady Bunch • (Meet) The Flintstones • Home Improvement • Mister Ed • Northern Exposure • This Is It (Bugs Bunny Theme) • Twin Peaks • and more.
00292030 ....$10.95

For More Information, See Your Local Music Dealer, Or Write To:

HAL•LEONARD® CORPORATION
7777 W. Bluemound Rd. P.O. Box 13819 Milwaukee, WI 53213

Visit Hal Leonard online at **www.halleonard.com**

Prices, contents, and availability subject to change without notice. Some products may not be available outside the U.S.A.